AS I WAS SAYING

AS I WAS SAYING

People Places and Things

Estelle Craig

authorHOUSE®

AuthorHouse™
1663 Liberty Drive
Bloomington, IN 47403
www.authorhouse.com
Phone: 1-800-839-8640

© 2012 by Estelle Craig. All rights reserved.

No part of this book may be reproduced, stored in a retrieval system, or transmitted by any means without the written permission of the author.

Published by AuthorHouse 03/09/2012

ISBN: 978-1-4685-4625-5 (sc)
ISBN: 978-1-4685-4626-2 (e)

Any people depicted in stock imagery provided by Thinkstock are models, and such images are being used for illustrative purposes only. Certain stock imagery © Thinkstock.

This book is printed on acid-free paper.

Because of the dynamic nature of the Internet, any web addresses or links contained in this book may have changed since publication and may no longer be valid. The views expressed in this work are solely those of the author and do not necessarily reflect the views of the publisher, and the publisher hereby disclaims any responsibility for them.

Contents

Topkapi 1
Only the Hardy Take Saunas 7
The Grand Duchess Olga 11
Don't Let Your Guide Be Your Conscience 14
The Duke of Bedford 19
My Friend Woody 23
Prime Minister Attlee 27
My Friend Victor 34
My Hat 37
My Balcony 39
Nina Prefers the Hula 43
Bali Bargain 48
The Fairy Tale Man 51
The White Witch 53
A Fairy Tale Tour 56
The Sun Hunters Club 60
Film Magic 65
Nuka Hiva 68
Moorea, French Polynesia 70
The Fabulous Rhine 73
Cairo 75
Calico Ghost Town (California) 79
Watch that Watch 82
Around the World on the Queen Mary 2 85

For Sheri, Collin and Robin
My Three Best Friends

Cover Graphics
by Robin

He came along
I was so young
He told me things
I liked to hear.
He whispered in my ear
To do things his way!

The day we wed
The things he said
He held me tight
It seemed so right
When we did it our way!

The years went by;
This nice big guy
Got older, too
And so did I
And so I'm left to
Do it my way.

The years have flown
I'm all alone
Except for those I've
Raised at home
I'm glad they're there
I know they care
When I do it my way!

Topkapi

JOHN HAD RED HAIR and could speak English fairly well. That was important. Not the red hair, particularly, but the English, since most of the other taxi drivers could not communicate. Besides, John had a vivacious personality and a pat sales talk. We had arrived in Istanbul only that morning, and John and the other taxi drivers were gathered near our cruise ship, hoping for business. The others waited, but John spoke up.

"I'll show you the city, the Blue Mosque, the Bazaar, anything you like. I'll show you the best shops," he said.

"But I want to see Topkapi Palace," I insisted. "Tomorrow is Tuesday and I was told it is always closed on Tuesdays. And our ship leaves here tomorrow night."

"Don't worry," John said. "I'll pick you up at your ship in the morning when the groups go. They open for groups. You buy your ticket and go in with the groups. Don't worry."

Estelle Craig

Our cruise had been delightful so far, and after Egypt, Istanbul was the place I wanted to see the most. With only a day and a half in port it was important to see the highlights, and of them all, Topkapi headed the list, for me anyway. It was Monday, and John said that since Topkapi would close in half an hour there was no point in rushing there now. So John had his way and off we went to the Blue Mosque. He waited outside, impatiently. The Bazaar was where he really wanted to go. He would show us the best places to buy. Even postcards and guide books were to be left to him. No one was to cheat us, he would see to that. As he drove, he remarked on the fabulous buys to be found at the Bazaar. Once there he steered me to what he claimed was the best jewelry shop in Istanbul.

"What you like?" he asked. What did I like? Everything. The saleslady said proudly that much of their stock came from Cartier in Paris. What did I want to see? I thought perhaps a coral pin might be nice. Pins were brought out. They were expensive and not quite what I had in mind. Then how about a coral ring? A jade ring? A diamond ring? No. I was decided. It had to be a coral pin or nothing. John was not happy. He disappeared. As I came out of the shop he reappeared and beckoned to me. He led me into another shop. "Good things in this shop," he said.

As I Was Saying

The owner of this store told me, rather than asked, what I wanted. "You want coral pin. We have best in Istanbul. Here you try." And he brought out everything he had in coral, bracelets, necklaces, but not the pin I thought I wanted.

"Lady, you try," he said. And before I could stop him he had fastened a lovely diamond and coral necklace around my neck.

"How much?" I asked timidly. It really was lovely.

"Cheap. Very cheap. For you special price. Only $2,500 US."

I gulped. It was hardly an inexpensive souvenir.

"That's a bit more than I had in mind," I said, turning to leave.

"Lady, I make you very good price." But I had escaped, only to find John propelling me into still another shop. As I walked down the Bazaar the shop owners came out at the sight of me. "Coral pin, you want coral pin, come and see beautiful pins." Up and down the Bazaar John had gone, like Paul Revere, announcing my coming and what I might want. But what I wanted was not there and I grew tired, I was disappointed, but not as disappointed as John. He would have received a commission on any purchase I made. Now he would only get his taxi fare. No wonder he was interested in letting me stop for postcards.

"Don't worry," he kept saying. "I show you the best place for postcards.

He had promised to come for me the next morning to drive me to Topkapi. He had been so talkative on the way to the Bazaar, but now he was silent on the way back to the ship. While I counted out his fare he suddenly announced that he had forgotten that he had another appointment for the following morning. He was sorry. He could not drive me to Topkapi. I understood. He preferred shoppers. I was not the shopper he could count on for a big commission. The next morning I arose early and went to find a taxi, not John's. Instead I found an honest driver.

"Topkapi," I asked hopefully.

"Maybe closed today, today Tuesday. Tuesday cleaning day Topkapi."

The ship was sailing that afternoon. I was desperate. "Let's go anyway," I said. Swiftly we drove to Topkapi, bypassing the Bazaar and other tourist places. But Topkapi was closed, guarded by two soldiers. My driver shook his head. It was hopeless, but I felt I had to try—The guards spoke no English, but one took pity on me and led me to the director of the museum. Yes, the palace was definitely closed for tourists on Tuesdays, but perhaps I might be able to see the exotic watch and clock collection, yes?

Oh, yes indeed. The director opened the building for me and there it was, an amazing assembly of diamond, jade and gold clocks belonging to Sultan Mehmet II who began the construction of Topkapi Palace after his conquest of Stamboul in 1453. While the Palace itself is in Europe it looks out on the continents of Europe and Asia from its peninsula surrounded on three sides by the waters of the Bosphorous, the Golden Horn and the Sea of Mamara.

It was time to go, but I was desolate. Could I just peek into the Treasury, the room where the famous emerald jewels and the equally famous jeweled dagger made world famous as the objective in the film "Topkapi?" Well, said the director, perhaps just for a moment. The cleaning men were busy washing the floor and we stepped gingerly over and around the mops. The men stared. No one ever came here on Tuesdays. But never mind, there were the jewels, and there was the dagger. Not on a figure, as in the film, but secure on the wall.

What a plot this would make, I thought. Here we were, only the director and me. No guards. Just the two of us and the dagger. I wondered if Hollywood would be interested in a story of someone breaking into Topkapi.

Only the Hardy Take Saunas

A SATURDAY NIGHT BATH in Finland is probably as ordinary and unglamorous as a Saturday night bath any place. But a sauna, now, that is totally different. It happened to me on a Monday night and I'll never get over it. We were on a tour of Finland in a little town some hundred or so miles from Helsinki. Our destination was a delightful hotel, equipped with its own sauna, which in Finland is a little wooden shack perched on the side of a lake. When our Finnish guide told me that a woman is at her most beautiful one hour after taking a sauna, I was determined to try one.

This sauna was ruled over by a little Finnish lady of advanced years. Her rule was law and she enforced it like a member of the Gestapo. She met me at the door of the shack with a contagious grin, enhanced by several missing teeth. We had no common language, but there was no misunderstanding her as she led me into the "undressing" room. I stripped and followed her into the "inferno" room, bare except for some wooden steps, two wooden benches at the top of the steps, and a furnace which kept the temperature at a minimum of 120 degrees and felt like 180.

"Sit," she commanded, pointing to the uppermost bench, the hottest spot in the room. I sat. Touching bare skin to bare bench I decided to lie down. Sitting was too much a chore. My general threw water on the stones. Beautiful steam surrounded us. She smiled happily, for it was getting even hotter. I decided to stop breathing, since this took too much effort. Then my friend reappeared, carrying a bucket of water and some birch branches, tied together. She gestured with the branches indicating that I was to dip them in water and slap my body with them. I tried, truly I did, but I could barely lift my arm, let alone the branches.

Then I heard the one word of English she knew. "Schwim," she ordered and pointed somewhere outside.

"Swim," I cried. "But it's almost midnight. The lake is too cold."

"Schwim," she ordered again, sternly. There was no way out, no way but the lake. She handed me a towel and guided me to the great outdoors. I dunked my toe in the water, and it was freezing. I had my towel draped around me for warmth, but the general tried to pull it away. I clutched it as firmly as I could. She tugged, I clutched. I won the battle of the towel but she won the bigger issue, the lake. I dunked my body and we marched back to the sauna.

The temperature inside was now hotter than I remembered, the branches seemed heavier to lift. I dripped, whether from the heat or the lake I didn't know and cared even less. More water was thrown on the stones to make it hotter and hotter and hotter. Finally it was time to "schwim" again. This time I dipped into the lake almost eagerly. Suddenly the air seemed warm, the water delightful. The moon danced as I swam, and I felt young and carefree.

Three times I sat in the sauna and three times went back to the lake. Finally I was summoned into another room where I was scrubbed down with soap and a brush strong enough to use on floors, even on horses. I never felt so clean in my life. I shone with health and baby pink complexion from head to toenail. On my way back to the hotel, the night air felt wonderfully warm, although I had needed my coat only a few hours earlier.

As I stood on the balcony outside my room I marveled at the feeling of no-night that prevails throughout Finland in the summer. I felt wonderful.

Estelle Craig

Now I knew why the Finns took their saunas so seriously. Then I remembered what my guide had said. This was the time a woman would look her very best. I turned to look in the mirror. Somehow it was still the same face. Oh well, saunas can do a lot, but they can't do everything.

The Grand Duchess Olga

THE GRAND DUCHESS OLGA was already there when I entered the room. She was sipping a cocktail, and I joined her after introductions were made. It was a beastly night, raining, windy and very cold. Olga, the Grand Duchess of Russia, seemed tiny and frail looking. She seldom went out, preferring seclusion in her country home. But when her good friend, Nicol Smith, called she couldn't resist. Neither could I. I had known Nicol for several years, and like most of his friends, when he called I usually accepted his invitation. This time it was to meet Olga, to join them for drinks at his hotel suite, and dinner later in the hotel dining room.

I never did find out how Nicol met Olga, but then he seemed to know everyone. He was the only child of Susie Smith, the one-time movie columnist for the Hearst newspaper chain. His father became a multi-millionaire after buying acres of land in northern California when land there was cheap as beans, and most people couldn't afford beans. Nicol was used to famous people, since his mother wrote about them all the time. Chatting with movie stars was an everyday occurrence So this cocktail party with Russian nobility was quite normal for him.

We drank, talked, laughed and finally had "one more for the road" at Nicol's suggestion, before proceeding down to the hotel dining room where he had reserved a large table. We formed ourselves into a procession as we marched slightly unsteadily into the dining room and to our table, watched with great interest by the other diners in the room. Nicol, who had earlier made a studied seating plan, held it up to his eyes. The light was dim, and he squinted, trying to make out where we were to be seated. Bad lighting and one drink too many, he gave up. We sat, wherever we happened to be. It was a fun dinner, a fun evening.

Almost a year later I received an invitation to the wedding of Olga's son, Prince Kulakowski. It was held at the Russian Orthodox Church in Toronto, and it was the most extraordinary wedding I have ever attended. The bride and groom stood at the head of a procession of six men. three behind the groom, three behind the bride. A crown was held over the heads of the bridal couple. When the first attendant's arm began to tire, the second attendant stepped forward to ensure that the crown did not fall. Then finally the third attendant took his place. The crowns never faltered.

There were no seats for the guests. We stood for the two hours of the ceremony. The Grand Duchess Olga, dressed in a simple cotton frock, stood by herself on a small mat near the altar. When the priest finished the rites, all the participants marched around the church three times. Then it was over. No refreshments were served. It was time to go home. I sent the prince a bone china cake plate as a wedding gift. It was so pretty that I bought one for myself. I still have mine. I don't think he has his, though, for he was divorced a few years later.

Don't Let Your Guide Be Your Conscience

TOURING EUROPE IS A sport indulged in by as many North Americans as there are seats on planes or standing room on ocean liners. It can be done on a shoestring/ ermine-lined, of course, or on a healthy budget of deluxe hotels where your dollars are more precious than pesatos, escudos or francs. But whatever kind of deal you arrange for yourself, package tour with everything taken care of, or "I'll go where I please and stay as long as I please" kind of arrangement, inevitably you must deal with a guide, somewhere.

Almost every North American who has been abroad for any length of time is approachable by a member of the "guide profession". And profession it is, for it concerns shopping concessions, contacts with wholesalers, guiding subcontracts and many other complicated sub-divisions of guiding that the innocent traveler is unaware of. Take, for example, Mr. Skiffleton, a guide I met in Morocco. Until ten years ago he was a native of California. A trip to Morocco, and perhaps an unwise past in California, inspired him to settle down there.

He is now one of the few Americans living in the Casbah, or Medina, as it is called by the Arabs.

Mr. Skiffleton makes his living from many sources, but officially he calls himself a guide. The financial gain from this is very small in comparison to his other businesses, for Mr. Skiffleton is a very resourceful man. In his capacity as guide he takes tourists to various points of interest, including the Medina, which is a must for anyone visiting Morocco.

Now, the Medina in Fez is at least 11 miles long and consists of incredibly narrow cobblestone streets along which file pedestrians, donkeys, filth and heat, not necessarily in that order. On either side of this street, which is approximately three feet wide, are stalls containing everything from the Arab delicacy, camelburger meat, to drapery material, Moroccan leather goods, jewelry of all descriptions, tables, jalabas, the traditional Arab robe and its accompanying red fez. Everything any tourist has ever seen or imagined.

Our Mr. Skiffleton has imagination. He realizes that he can easily guide his tourists into one stall, and bypass another. And he does just that, after first making arrangements with as many shopkeepers as will give him a good commission. Naturally, the better the commission, the higher on the list are the stalls to be visited. The tourists are guided along the Medina with eyes as big as their pocketbooks, looking at the natives and the articles displayed. You name it, everything is for sale. The tourists, most of them women, appeal to Mr. Skiffleton to take them into a shop, the best shop. Little do they realize that this is exactly what Mr. Skiffleton has been planning for them, and every tourist he can get into the Medina!

The group passes a stall crammed with lovely copper trays, vases, leather work, jewelry. The ladies cry with delight. This is a good shop, says their guide. Would they like to come in? Would they, indeed. The ladies, few men in the group reluctantly following, enter the shop, with Mr. Skiffleton whispering cautiously, "Now, don't pay what they ask. I'll bargain them down for you." This makes him their very good friend, obviously on their side.

He does bargain down for them, too, but what the customer doesn't always know is that the original asking price is much higher than it should be, and that the eventual selling price is what the shopkeeper hoped to get and was prepared to go even lower, if necessary. What the customer doesn't know, too, is that Mr. Skiffleton has originally imported the article himself and has sold it to the shopkeeper, so that he has a two-fold interest in seeing to it that his tourists go into that particular shop.

He is a good actor, this Mr. Skiffleton, because even though he is anxious for as many sales as possible, he assumes an air of complete indifference as to the outcome of the sale. This makes his group of tourists respect him, and they feel that he doesn't give a hoot whether they buy or not. The fact is, he does care terribly, for although guiding may pay for his bread and butter, the extra commissions pay for his meat, wine and caviar.

In Spain we met a guide without quite as much imagination, but with enough ingenuity to guide us into a "special factory" where, we were told, mantillas are made. It is impossible for a woman to visit Spain and return without a mantilla, so even though it was Sunday and all the stores were closed, Horace "used his influence" and guided us right into the factory. The mantillas were higher priced than we had expected, but we had to have them, and Horace sat carefully by, noting our purchases in his little notebook. Since we were impressed with Horace's ability to get us into this factory, we felt obligated to buy, and the mantillas and lace handkerchiefs that returned to Toronto with us, to remain forever unused, are countless. But we knew, without being told, that Horace would return to the factory after we left for his commissions on our purchases, tabulated in neat figures for a neat profit, in addition to his guiding fee.

Simon was more discreet. Simon knew Portugal well, including the names of all the trees, flowers and livestock, and loved them all. Simon seemed to care less about shopping and commissions, but was businesslike enough to mention some of the better shops if we cared to buy anything. It may indeed have been a coincidence that one of the recommended shops belonged to his brother, but it was a pleasant thought that his family would benefit from our shopping. He did manage, we later discovered, to make an extra escudo or two, by promising to mail letters and postcards, when stamps were unavailable, as they often were.

"Just leave them with me," he promised. "I will mail them for you." Alas, poor Simon found no stamps, but pocketed the money and tips for his task, instead. The letters were never mailed!

Today it is no longer the question of how much the tourists overpay, but who they overpay. We couldn't have had nicer guides to find this out.

The Duke of Bedford

IT WAS A FUN day from morning to night. In fact it was a fun day and two fun weeks before it happened. I had booked the Duke of Bedford for a lecture in Toronto, following the publishing of his new book "A Silver-Plated Spoon,"! I thought I would have a huge audience, since Toronto in the late'50s was turned on to anything that had to do with royalty, the nobility or upper class British. In fact I had seriously considered booking Massey Hall, at that time the largest auditorium available, seating 2750. Logic prevailed, and I resorted to my usual theatre, Eaton Auditorium. For some unknown reason ticket sales were extremely sluggish and I realized I would have to do something to stimulate sales.

So one day, when I knew the Duke had left London for his lecture tour, I called the Telegram, The Star and The Globe & Mail, the three largest Toronto newspapers, and told them that I had just heard from the Duke and he had advised me that he was interested in buying Casa Loma. In fact he didn't even know there was a Casa Loma. That evening, in big bold headlines, the papers screamed that the Duke was coming to buy Casa

Loma, the only castle in North America, and a great tourist attraction.

The following day all the papers had editorials talking about the possible purchase. There were cartoons showing the Duke at home in Casa Loma. Another showed the Mayor on the ramparts of Casa Loma, defending it from the Duke who was approaching it on his horse. He was dressed in armor, and looked ferocious. There were many articles proclaiming that Casa Loma never never should be sold, especially to the Duke who, they said, would turn it into a carnival.

The Kiwanis Club, which was running Casa Loma as a charitable enterprise, called me to say that there was no way they would sell it, but as a courtesy they would show the Duke around the building. My husband and my son were horrified at what I had done, so I called the Duke's agent. She suggested that I speak with the Duke before the newspapers got hold of him. I expected the Duke in the night before the lecture, and had booked a hotel room for him. I called the hotel and asked that he call me when he arrived, regardless of the hour.

When he called I explained what I had done, and why I had done it. He thought it most amusing and went along with the game. The following morning I had a huge press conference for him at a breakfast at the hotel, which was attended by all of the media. When he was asked about Casa Loma and how he had heard about it he said some fellow, somewhere, had told him about it. Unfortunately, during the press conference he received a phone call from London from his wife, telling him that she was divorcing him. This was in front of the press, diverting more talk about his lecture that evening.

Ticket sales did not increase by much, but the fun did. After the press conference was over we drove to Casa Loma, where the president of Kiwanis and his executives were waiting for us. TV cameras followed us through the building and we had a thorough tour. The Duke was presented with the castle souvenirs and we left. When we dropped him off at the hotel he refused to take the souvenirs, which were a salt and pepper set, in the form of a castle, made in Japan, and a toy bank, also made in Japan. That evening I did not have a capacity audience, but the audience was thrilled at his talk. He was extremely amusing. After the lecture we went to a supper club where a well-known comedian was appearing.

When I reserved a table I mentioned that the Duke was to be my guest. When we arrived at the supper club the comedian, Jack Carter, was in the middle of one of his routines. He saw us enter, and immediately changed his routine to include mention of the Duke. Later he came over to our table, to greet the Duke, Ian, as he asked to be called. And a bit later the Duke was called out into the lobby. The next day his picture was in all the papers, pouring champagne into a slipper, held by the hat check girl. As he intimated, he would do anything for publicity. And he did.

Bedford, Ian, to his friends, looked more like a banker than a titled landowner. His home, which I visited, was a mansion set in the midst of hundreds of acres of expensive land. Taxes were high. The Duke had inherited the property and was determined to keep it. So he inaugurated a number of tourist attractions which did indeed bring many tourists to his castle. He even included a tour of part of his home, the ground floor, where portraits of many of his ancestors flanked the halls and the walls of many of the rooms. The dining room was enormous and its table was laid with rich silver service. Seeing all this I understood the Duke's real need for money, and his highly developed flair for publicity, the only way to bring in the crowds.

My Friend Woody

SOME TIME AGO THE Globe & Mail published a letter from a woman who blamed her parents for not telling her what her life would be like when she reached her eighties. No one can experience life for some one else. It's all trial and error. Some endure the trials, others fall by the wayside. Advanced age (why call it old age?) should be just that. Advanced with the maturity we should have developed by then, advanced through lessons learned, advanced through the joy of being.

So when I reached those "golden years" and the days seemed to be getting longer and the nights stretched on forever I realized I was feeling lonely, I thought I better do something about it. After living alone for five years, I came to the reality, after my husband's death, that I needed something, someone. So I bought a dog. It was either a dog or a baby, and at my age who needs a baby? I really didn't want a dog either. But I was lonely, and my children said, "If you have a dog and go for a walk, people will start talking to you."

I asked. "Will they talk to me or my dog?"

They said. "What difference does it make? At least there will be someone there you can talk to."

Now don't misunderstand me, it wasn't always like this. I used to have friends. Lots of friends. I had a husband, too. It's true he didn't talk very much, but he was there, and even if he didn't talk I could talk to him. But one by one they all died. Just took off. I couldn't believe they would do this to me. What had I done to deserve it? After all, I gave them the best years of my life. And their lives, too. Well, anyway, here I am. The baby is definitely out. So I bought a dog.

I decided to get a Retriever. I figured if I dropped anything the dog would retrieve it for me. A Retriever should be able to retrieve. We shopped around for just the right dog. He had to blend in with my furniture, be well mannered and know when and where to go to the bathroom. Also I wanted to be sure we were compatible. After all, you don't take just anyone into your home. We rejected quite a few dogs and then I saw him. He had deep set brown eyes and looked as lonely as I felt. Right away I knew we were meant for each other. I called him Woody and he called me Woof. We were a pair.

I bought Woody a bed and a genuine leather leash. I figured if he didn't work out, I could use the leash as a belt. Then we did a few practice turns around the block. And finally we were ready to visit the park and to meet people. People who would become my new friends. Maybe a woman or two. Maybe even a man. Not that I was looking for romance. No. not really. Actually I was thinking in terms of someone who might be a great escort when we went out for dinner or even (gulp) dining and dancing on occasion. Woody, I said to my dog, bring me luck.

Well, we ventured into the park and I could see that Woody was really attracting attention. He is handsome, walking with his nose up in the air like the aristocrat that he thinks he is, instead of running around, sniffing other dogs' rumps. Then I saw two women talking to each other while their dogs played nearby. I walked over to them and said, "Your dogs seem to know each other. I'd like them to meet Woody. Is that okay?"

They looked at each other and one of them said, "That's up to the dogs." So I gave Woody a little shove in the dogs' direction and told him to go play with his new friends. I said to the women, "Woody is new around here. I would like to make him feel comfortable. I don't want him to be lonely. That's not good for man or beast. Or woman either."

Well, we began to talk and I told them why I got the dog. And I think my children were right. Look at me, I'm talking to people I don't even know. Then out of the corner of my eye I saw him. He was walking his dog. He was tall, and from the way he walked I knew he was a good dancer. So I said goodbye to the two women and pulled Woody away from his new friends. It was time for Woody to meet another friend. And time for me to meet someone who might turn out to be more than a friend. I can introduce Woody to his dog and myself to him. If we don't have much to say to each other maybe the dogs will develop a deep friendship. You never know.

Prime Minister Attlee

WHEN I RECEIVED WORD that ex-Prime Minister Attlee of England was about to start off on a lecture tour I was intrigued. Toronto is, or was, so very pro-British, I thought, and people would certainly come out in droves to see and hear this man. I booked him, although his fee was higher than I was accustomed to pay. But I wasn't really worried. I was certain that I would have a large audience, and with that in mind I booked Massey Hall, which seated 2750, instead of my usual theatre which seated 1264.

From time to time I would read about Attlee's tour, where he was speaking, and what he was speaking about. He seemed to be speaking mostly before service and private clubs, and his subject seemed to be about the social economy of the last part of the 19th century. The reviews were not very good, and I became worried, for this would be a very expensive evening for me if tickets did not sell well. I had been given a choice of several topics for Attlee to speak on, but in every instance I read about, he talked only about the economy of the end of the 19th century.

Estelle Craig

The contract I had signed with his New York agent specified that I requested that he was to come to Toronto two to three weeks prior to his lecture here for a press conference. I thought good press would stimulate interest in him and produce better ticket sales. Accordingly, when the time came he flew in and I met him and his wife at the airport and drove them into town for the press conference I was holding for him the next day. It was a cold, snowy evening, it was late at night, so we left our car outside the terminal building while we went in to collect the Attlees and help them through Customs and Immigration. We drove them to their hotel, and the next day at the press conference, which was attended by almost everyone in the media, he was asked many questions about conditions in England. His only answer was "I really don't know. I haven't been there in a fortnight." I was mortified at his responses. He had few answers for any questions asked. Ticket sales were bad. The articles in the press the next day did not show him in a good light. I became convinced that I must try to cancel his speaking engagement.

When I had first booked him I had called the Mayor's office to suggest that the city welcome Attlee in some manner. The Mayor agreed to have a dinner party for him, and asked me to help make up a list of guests. I told Attlee about the dinner and he said he would be pleased to attend. But when I thought about the small amount of ticket sales, I continued to think it would be best to cancel. I was worried. I called the booking agency in New York and told them that Attlee seemed to have only one subject, that he was not going to speak on the subject agreed in my contract with him, and that I would have to cancel since tickets were not selling, and his press was not good. I was asked if I would speak to Attlee if he phoned me, and that he would tell me himself that he would speak on the agreed subject. The next day Attlee called and said he understood I was unhappy with ticket sales. I replied that unless he could guarantee that he would speak on the subject I had requested, I would have to cancel. He hemmed and hawed and I could sense he didn't have a clue as to the problem. I thanked him for calling and hung up.

Then I called the Massey Hall manager to see if I could be released from my contract there. Not only did he release me, with no penalty, but he advised me to cancel the lecture. I then called my lawyer, and he also advised me to cancel. He said the agency might sue me, but if I did go ahead with the lecture show, I would be obliged to pay Attlee his full fee, plus the cost of the hall, plus all the advertising I would have to do. He advised me to take my chances that I would not be sued.

Then I called the New York agency and told them I had gotten nowhere with Attlee, that he would not guarantee to speak on what I had requested, and that I was advising them that I was about to cancel his engagement. The agency people were furious and said they would sue me. That night the phones began to ring at my house with calls from all over the world. Somehow, and I don't know how, word had gotten out that I had cancelled the Prime Minister of England. That seemed to be shocking news. The Toronto newspapers printed front page stories about this, and my sister, who lived in Manhattan, read about it in her newspaper. I had already paid for some advertising and printing of fliers, but that is all the money I lost. If I had not cancelled I would have lost over $6,000.

The next day I had a furious phone call from the Mayor, who said, "What have you done to my dinner party?" I told him I had nothing to do with Attlee any more and he could do as he liked about the dinner. He said I was responsible for it, and it would go on, as scheduled. A few days later I had another call from Attlee, asking if he could still come to the dinner. On the day he was to arrive, I had another call from the Mayor, telling me he wanted me to go out to the airport to meet and greet the Attlees. I refused and said I had nothing to do with the dinner or Attlee any more. I was told I was responsible for the dinner and I had to go out to the airport and represent Toronto for the Mayor, since he could not go himself.

As I Was Saying

When the appointed day arrived I asked my husband to drive out with me. We had a brand new Lincoln Continental in a beautiful maroon shade, but I had only driven it once or twice. My husband refused to come, so I called the British Trade Minister and invited him to come to the airport with me. I knew if the press got wind of me going to meet the man I had cancelled, they would have a field day. The British Trade Minister and his wife came with me, in my car, since their car was quite small. When we arrived at the airport I parked in front, just as we had done when we went the night before the press conference. I told the Trade Minister I would wait in the entrance, where I wouldn't be seen by any lurking photographers or reporters, while he went to get the Attlees. It took some time before they came out, and when I saw them I joined them. We went to where I had parked the car, but it was not there. I searched everywhere. It had been towed away. I had to wade through mounds of snow, without boots, to the place where they had towed it, pay a fine, and drive back for them The next day there was a front page story in the newspapers about the Prime Minister's car being towed away. I had not told my husband about this. He was not amused.

We drove back to the Trade Minister's house, and were invited in for tea. It was getting late and I knew I had to drive the Attlees back to their hotel, drive myself home, feed my children, and change clothes for the big dinner the Mayor had insisted I attend. When the Minister offered the Attlees a second cup of tea I told them we didn't have time for that. We had to leave. Now. At once. Just before leaving Attlee was asked if he wanted to borrow a pair of boots. He tried on several pair before selecting one. And then we left.

Now, for the first time since I cancelled him, I was alone with the Attlees. I knew they weren't happy with me, but I was even more unhappy with them. Mrs. Attlee was very snippy and quite unpleasant with everyone around her. Trying to make conversation on the drive, when we passed some nice shops I told her she might like to look in on them. She replied, "Oh, we don't have any money for me to shop."

I was delighted to leave them at their hotel and started for home. It was rush hour, and I thought if I managed to get straight home I might be able to do everything that needed to be done, and leave for the dinner in time. Suddenly, in the middle of traffic, the car stalled. I noticed that the gas gauge pointed to empty. But before leaving the house I had asked my husband if there was enough gas in the car, and he assured me there was.

So there I was, in the middle of traffic in a stalled car. Finally, I got another car to push me over to a curb, where I found a phone nearby. I called home, but my husband said he knew there was enough gas in the car. I went back, and again tried to start the car. It was no use. I called home again, and said I would call a service station to tow the car in. It was getting very late, and I was getting no place. My husband said to wait, and he would come. He was sure he could start the car. So he took my small car and came flying down to where I was. Of course he couldn't start it and we ended up calling a service station to tow the car away.

We hurried home, and while I was changing for the dinner we kept getting calls from the Mayor's office. Where was I? They were waiting dinner for me. We did get to the dinner. Attlee did speak, and he was good, and he was funny. If he had spoken like that on the lecture circuit he would have been a smash and I would not have cancelled him. And the car? It was out of gas. Of course.

My Friend Victor

I MET VICTOR THROUGH a mutual friend, who had advised me to call Victor when I arrived in Stockholm. Victor was curator of a museum, and a native of Stockholm. "Call him," she said. "He will take you around and show you the sights." So when I arrived in Sweden I did call Victor. He came over to my hotel, and after chatting for awhile he asked if I would like to take a walk. I agreed and we walked for a great distance until we reached his museum. It was after hours, but he had his keys and we entered the magnificent building where the Nobel Prize is presented. We were the only two people in the building, and I was free to wander about, even sit on the King's throne. It was a thrilling experience.

I started my tour of the Scandinavian countries in Norway, but my husband had not been able to get away then and was to meet me in Stockholm. So when he arrived the next day, I introduced him to Victor. The three of us spent days together, seeing the sights through the eye of a native who knew his stuff. The days flew by and it was time to leave. So when we saw Victor for the last time, it seemed like the polite thing to do. After all, we had spent three whole days with him, sometimes including lunch and dinners every night.

He took us places we would never have seen, if it hadn't been for Victor. Of course we did our best to repay him, but no money was exchanged and by this time we had become good friends. So when it became time for us to leave Stockholm, and Victor, we told him how much we had enjoyed our time spent with him. Then impulsively I added, "And if you are ever in Toronto do let us know." And with that we left Victor and continued on our tour.

After visiting Denmark and Finland we returned to Toronto with wonderful memories of our trip, especially our time with Victor in Sweden. The day after we returned home, while I was unpacking our luggage, the phone rang. It was Victor.

"How nice to hear from you" I said. "Where are you?"

"I'm in Toronto. Can I come to see you today?" Victor asked.

"Well, Victor, of course we would like to see you," I told him, "But we only just returned home last night. I'm unpacking our things now. Can you wait until tomorrow?"

"Yes, I can wait until tomorrow. I will see you then."

So Victor came to our house the next day, and the next day, and the next day. He came every day and he always came around five thirty. We usually had dinner at six o'clock. We felt it would not be polite for us to sit down at the table while Victor was there. So we had to invite him to join us. This went on, night after night for over two weeks. At five thirty every night there was Victor. My husband became angry.

"Tell him not to come here anymore," he demanded.

I replied, "You tell him."

Neither one of us had the courage to confront Victor, who seemed to think our house was his castle, too. He had found an apartment near our place, but was not successful at finding a job.

The atmosphere at home was beginning to become unpleasant. We didn't know what to do about Victor. And then my husband had a brilliant idea. He decided to lend Victor some money. And that did the trick. Victor took the money and we never saw or heard from him again. So now when I meet someone new, even if I like them, I never say "if you are ever in Toronto, do call us." Because I'm afraid they will.

My Hat

I BOUGHT A HAT one day, something I had done in the past, many many times. But this time it was different. This was a hat that might have been worn by a queen. Not Queen Elizabeth. She wasn't the type. Maybe Diana. But I didn't know about her then. For this was a long time ago, maybe forty years ago and Diana wasn't even born yet No, this was a hat that Rita Hayworth would have worn, or even Marlene Dietrich, but it would have looked better on Rita.

I had been involved in several theatrical productions for a few years and decided to put on a special show apart from the series. For this the people would have to pay, not that much, but a bit extra. It was very successful, and I cleared over one thousand dollars for that one night, all expenses paid. That was a lot of money then, and I felt pretty good about my judgment, my series and the world. Yes, I felt really good. And then I passed a millinery store. You must remember that we all wore hats then. Hats and usually gloves. And here was this hat, in the window, and it spoke to me. It said, "I am yours, buy me". So I went in and asked for the hat, and it was $60.00, which was enough for a family to feed on in those days, for an entire week. I tried the hat on, and it looked so good on me. But I knew it would. I knew it had been made for me. I had to have it. After all, I had just made $1000 on a gamble.

I may have worn the hat twice, certainly not much more. It was made of white panne velvet, trimmed with gold lame and worked into a turban. My usual outings were to Loblaw supermarkets and I knew my hat didn't belong there. Other outings were to friends' homes for dinner or bridge. Occasionally I would remove it from its box and try it on. It always made me feel good. But when we decided to move, I found there was no room for nostalgia. Crippled Civilians came and took my hat away. I wonder who got it. Did she love it the way I did? Anyway, we don't wear hats any more.

My Balcony

I HAVE SAVED MY balcony for myself this year. For the past two years I have been a prisoner of my own making. I have a large balcony overlooking a ravine and a glimpse of Lake Ontario. On a clear day you can see almost forever. For the few precious months one can enjoy warm sitting-out-doors weather in Toronto, I really do want to enjoy them. I also like to pretend I have a garden, so I plant flowers and put up hanging baskets.

Two years ago I hung a basket of lovely flowers, and a few weeks later noticed I was having company. Two little strangers were inspecting my quarters. The male bird was the noisy one, commenting to his mate on what he saw. He was brilliantly attired in a red vest and a long red tail. The female looked drab beside him. She spoke hardly a word. I figured she must have quite a personality for him to choose her. Not really ugly, but certainly not sexy looking. They left after a while, and the next day they were back, bringing twigs and bits and pieces of greenery to my hanging plant, where they proceeded to build a nest. This went on for quite a while. I was fascinated. I forgot to do my chores. I forgot to go out. I almost considered calling in an architect friend to see if he approved of their house plans.

They stole moss and foliage from one of my favorite plants. Every day I would push the moss down into the plant only to find it pulled out again the next day. The wrens, for that is what the birds were, are new to this part of Canada. Now at last they had their dream house, and it was time to start their family. Mr. Wren sat on the balcony ledge and sang to his love while she was occupied in the nest. Then she would emerge and they would fly away together, and return together the next day. I was dying of curiosity, Did she really lay the eggs? How many? What did they look like? So one evening when they went off I climbed up on a chair and peered into the nest. The nest was beautifully constructed, a true work of art. In the nest were six tiny blue eggs. I was thrilled and planned to welcome them to my home.

From that time on I refused to let anyone on to the balcony. The days were long, sunny and warm. No matter. They were not to be enjoyed by anyone in this house. These were my birds, and I was determined to protect them. So I stayed home to watch the wrens come and go. Appointments were cancelled. I knew now what was important. It was those tiny blue eggs. When Mrs. Wren finally spent all her time in the nest I almost climbed in with her, I was so excited. The great day finally came, and a little fellow came tumbling out of the nest, hit the floor and staggered around. Then another came out, and then a third. Mother Wren stood by, observing, then proceeded to give them flying lessons. She hopped from floor to chair, to table, back to floor. They did the same thing. Then mother, father and their babies flew away together. It took several more days before the other birds emerged. Each time the parents were there to escort them someplace. I don't know where.

Now the best part of the summer was gone. The weather had turned cooler, my nice plant was ruined, my birds had left me, and I had been under virtual house arrest because I did not want to leave them. Balcony time was over. Last year I bought another hanging basket. I was so sure the wrens would not remember me. No sooner was it up when they returned, same red vest and tail, same little wife. Now the pattern was repeated, they flew, he sang, they built their nest, they mated, she sat, he sang loud and long. I waited and waited, cooped up again. I admit I was still fascinated by all this activity, left beds unmade, dishes unwashed, waiting for the chicks to emerge. I wanted to see another flying lesson. I must have missed it, somehow, or maybe these new chicks were smarter and didn't need any lessons. But when the Wren family left I heaved a a sigh of relief.

Estelle Craig

This year there will be no hanging basket. I want my balcony back. But now that I have it, it has been so cold I can't sun bathe. Perhaps I really should invite the wrens back. They surely brought good weather with them.

Nina Prefers the Hula

"THE KIDS HERE," SAID Nina, "don't want to do the hula any more. They would rather do rock and roll. Them kids! They won't even speak Hawaiian, even at home. They tell me I'm old-fashioned when I talk to them in Hawaiian". Nina was our driver, in a big Cadillac, on the island of Maui. She wore the traditional muumuu, sandals on her feet, and a huge red hibiscus caught in her hair. I had never seen a driver-guide quite like Nina before. Big and buxom, no one could even hazard a guess as to her correct size or weight. The muumuu is a long sack-like dress, disguising good and bad figures alike. Only when Nina walked could one surmise that she did, indeed, need the disguise afforded by the muumuu.

We were talking on the long drive up the mountain to visit the giant Haleakala Crater, the largest dormant crater in the world. The road was winding and narrow. Parts of it were wide enough for only one car. Nina kept blowing her horn to warn on-coming motorists, and I kept my foot on an imaginary brake to stop the car quickly if it should become necessary. Nina didn't mind my help or the impossible road. She tended to her business, driving with her sandal-shod feet and answering my questions.

"Nina, do you like Maui better than the other islands?"

"Well, I live here, and I like it all right. But I was born on the Big Island. I love it there. You should see the flowers we grow there. And it's always sunny and dry and warm there, all year 'round."

I assured Nina that I would indeed see the Big Island. We were going there the very next day, having spent a few days on Maui. But how any island could be an improvement over Maui was difficult to imagine. Second largest of the Hawaiian Island group, it did not have the touristy aspect of Honolulu. Commercialism, apart from the pineapple and sugar cane industry, had not yet invaded the place. People like Nina were dependant on tourists like myself, and were earning more and more there these last few years. But not enough yet to have spoiled the island. There were a few very good hotels, and one of the most exclusive hotels would not accept guests who would not stay at least five days.

The male drivers assigned to our group had tried to discourage us from taking the long trip up to Haleakala Crater. It was misty, they said, and we would not be able to see anything. Only rarely did the clouds lift, and this very morning four cars had driven up and returned with the sad news that they had indeed seen nothing. But we were determined, and so was Nina.

"Them men," she said, "they're just lazy. Come on, I'll take you."

It was worth the trip, just to talk to Nina. Her family lived in a camp, she explained. Her husband, of Irish-Hawaiian descent, worked in the sugar cane fields where the camp was located. Eventually, the camp houses would be eliminated and low-cost houses would be substituted for the workers and their families. Meanwhile, the salary her husband made and her own income, earned by driving tourists during the season, was quite satisfactory.

Were the youngsters leaving the island? Yes, Nina explained, because there were no jobs for them. Her own son was now attending high school. Soon he would go to Honolulu to take the course at the university. Would he come back to Maui? Probably not, Nina admitted. There was really nothing to come back to.

We had reached the summit by now, 10,000 feet up, and the wind was blowing unmercifully. Racing from the car we took refuge in the glass-enclosed cabin perched on the edge of the crater. It was misty, and hard to believe we were in beautiful warm Hawaii. Clouds were everywhere. Then, as if by magic, as we stood peering out, the curtains of mystery parted and there was the crater, magnificent in its starkness of red, brown and gray stone, with evidences of greenery and the growth of shrubbery that one would find at the bottom of the crater. Twenty-seven miles around the rim of the crater, three thousand feet deep, it was incredibly big and forbidding. Yet, even now, Nina said, some people were camping down below.

Just as suddenly as the clouds had lifted, they were back now, and there was nothing to see, only the mist and the sound of the winds. We returned to the car for the ride back to the hotel, considering ourselves lucky to have had this glimpse of the crater, however brief. On the way back, Nina pointed out the Silver Sword Plant, which grows nowhere else in the world but at this elevation on the island of Maui. I wanted to stop and look at it, this rarity, and perhaps pluck a bit to bring home with me.

"Oh, no," said Nina, driving past furiously. "You pick that, you pay five hundred dollar fine, and go to jail for six months."

Much as I enjoyed Maui, I decided it was too expensive a way to spend my time there. We passed the jail, and Nina pointed it out.

"That's the most luxurious hotel on the island," she chuckled. "Got a bar in every room."

Was she impressed with Hawaii becoming the 50th State? Did she vote in the election?

Nina grunted. "Vote? Not me, any more. I used to vote when it was fun. We used to have luaus every night. People would come call for you in their car, take you to vote, then take you to the luau. There would be singing and we'd do the hula. And the food, it was dee-licious. Now election day is just like any other day. Sure I'm glad we're a state now. Be good for us. But give me back the good old days, and I'll vote again."

Bali Bargain

HE WAS PROBABLY TEN or twelve years old. His eyes twinkled as he held up the ivory carvings. "Fi dollah, lady. Fu you." News of our arrival had reached the natives, and they were out in full force trying to sell their wares. They had all sorts of souvenirs, necklaces, batik cloths and ivory carvings. Most of the natives surrounding us were women and children, but none of them were as persistent as this little fellow.

"Only fi' dollah, lady," he kept saying.

"No thank you," we said repeatedly, trying to escape. But he refused to accept this. He followed us closely. He waited outside the washroom. He followed us back to the bus, plucking at our sleeve.

"Lady, you buy my ivory. Only fi' dollah. Very fine ivory."

"No, I don't want it, thank you."

"Lady, how 'bout four dollah?"

As I Was Saying

"No. No, no, no. Please go away. I don't want it."

Safe on the bus the youngster tried to follow us on. The bus driver stopped him and closed the door. But the windows were open. The lad was as determined as ever. He continued his salesmanship through the window.

"Lady, how 'bout two dollah?" I shook my head.

"Lady, how 'bout two dollah for two ivories?" Now this was indeed a tremendous bargain. They seemed to be well carved, from what I could see. They looked to be real ivory. I reached out to examine them, and he grinned and handed them to me through the window. The other passengers on the bus watched curiously. The carvings weren't great, but they were carved nicely, and would be a pleasing reminder of my trip to Bali. Two dollars for the two? How could I refuse!

"All right," I said. "I'll take them." His face broke into a huge smile.

"I wrap them for you," he said. He bent down to get a paper bag and I gave him the money as he handed me my purchase. He waved as the bus started on its way. That was certainly a great buy, I thought.

But was it? I decided to examine the ivories again, and opened the parcel. These ivories were all chipped, and one was broken so badly it had to be thrown away. The little imp had switched the ivories while he was putting them in the paper bag. Yes, I had gotten a bargain, or so I thought, but he had won the battle of wits.

The Fairy Tale Man

HE WASN'T HANDSOME, AND if he cared no one knew it. He always wore a silk top hat, and traveled with two canes and a rope, along with his ever-present umbrella. The king of Denmark had given him one of his canes, and he was proud of it. But he would rather have parted with it then leave his rope behind. His name was Hans Christian Anderson, and he was terribly afraid of fire. Therefore the rope was necessary, and when he stayed at hotels on his trips he would immediately go up to his room after checking in and lower the rope outside his room to see exactly how high up he was. If the rope reached the ground he knew he was safe, and he would leave it dangling outside his window in case of fire so that he could descend quickly, if necessary. Of course, there never was a fire, and he never had to use the rope. But there it was, just the same.

I met Hans Christian Anderson's spirit while on a "fairy land tour" in the lesser known parts of Denmark. It was almost like reading his fairy tales, in this enchanting world of little white houses with storks nesting on chimney tops, thatched roof farms, moated castles and mermaids. History became fact as buildings dating back to the 12th century came into view. Here were beautiful manor houses and castles, and at Eageskov, one of the most beautiful in all of Denmark, built in 1550 on oak piles rammed into a lake bed, one could almost hear the loud sobbing of the daughter walled up in the castle by her wrathful father. This is where Anderson lived, in this Denmark of castles and fairy land, and this is where his wonderful imagination conjured up his famous tales.

The man who wanted to be known as a poet has his very own museum at Odense where people come to pay homage, see his birthplace, buy souvenirs and reread his stories. If you study his stories carefully you realize that grammatically they are not perfect. But the charm is there, along with his unhappiness as a child, even as a man, when he loved many women who did not love him in return. And each time he felt his love affair was coming to an end he would pick up his two canes, his umbrella, his top hat and his rope, and go off on another trip, to forget.

The White Witch

WE SAT ON THE old steps of Rose Hall, Amariah Denham and I, and discussed the Legend of the White Witch. Here, in Montego Bay, Jamaica, over 150 years ago, Annie Palmer lived, killed and was in turn murdered by her servants. Since then she has reportedly haunted her home, Rose Hall, and thus gave birth to the Legend of the White Witch.

I came to visit Amariah, who has been caretaker at Rose Hall for the past forty years. He knows more about Rose Hall than almost any other person in Jamaica. "When I was a boy of 14," he told me, "I walked through the house and saw bloodstains left from the killing of Annie Palmer." He pronounced it "Ahnnie" in his soft Jamaican drawl that was such a pleasure to listen to, but sometimes left me wondering whether I understood his words correctly.

"Ahnnie married three times," he continued, "and killed all of her husbands." There was a servant she was enamored of, who was also loved by Annie's maid. One day they decided to end Annie's cruelty, and killed their mistress. Her screams were dreadful, and perhaps in revenge she has haunted the house and grounds since that time. Today, Rose Hall stands, a shell of the beautiful mansion it once was, with its magnificent mahogany staircase, huge polished brass locks and exotic furnishings. Once the finest and costliest of mansions, today it is eerie and brooding as it stands alone, high on a hill, visited only by tourists who come hoping to see the ghost of Annie Palmer.

Amariah is a dark, sincere man, devoted to the house and the legend. "Did you ever see any evidence of the place being haunted?" I asked. "Yes, I did," said Amariah. "One evening over near the east end of the house, nearby where Ahnnie is buried, I saw a white hearse."

I looked east toward a pile of stones, marking the site of Annie's grave. I shivered. "A white hearse, are you sure?"

"Yes, lady, I'm sure. A white hearse, with someone in it."

"Was it a dead person?" I asked.

"Well, I didn't know then, but later when I told the overseer about it, he said I was lucky to have seen it. Not many people have."

"Was it Annie?"

"Yes, it must have been. She had on her riding clothes."

Now, that sounded odd, a dead person in a hearse, wearing riding clothes. Still, I'm not exactly sure of the habits of ghosts. I accepted Denham's word, and we went on to discuss Annie's peculiar ways. She made her servants carry quantities of water daily from the sea to her private swimming pool, some great distance away. She took successions of lovers, killing most of them in her ever increasing lunacy and nymphomania. No one, except perhaps Rose Hall itself, mourned her passing.

I said goodbye to Amariah and walked back to our car. I mentioned the story Amariah had told me of his vision, and my driver vouched for his accuracy. But when I repeated the tale of the hearse, the driver was skeptical. "Hearse," he wondered. "He probably meant a horse, a white horse." He did indeed for when I went back to verify this Amariah said, "Of course I saw a hearse, a white hearse," meaning, of course, a horse.

There are at present plans afoot to restore Rose Hall as it once was, and the property around it has been bought. It will become a golf course, with the mansion as a club house. Golfers who are duds can surely blame Annie Palmer.

A Fairy Tale Tour

THE ENCHANTED WORLD OF fairy land becomes a reality on a Fairy Tale Tour of Denmark, unknown to many travelers who think of Denmark in terms of Copenhagen and a look at Tivoli Gardens. Tivoli is a wondrous place, a gigantic garden of amusements, flowers, lights and a paradise for children. But for a "stars in the eyes" expression lasting during the three days of the Fairy Tale Tour, this is one trip a family can take together, with adults and children alike delighted with discoveries.

Fairy Tale Land is the "unexplored" part of Denmark, and is reached by a comfortable bus boarded at Copenhagen. We found the bus filled, but not uncomfortably so, with people wanting to see the Denmark that inspired Hans Christian Anderson's wonderful fairytales. Our guide was a dark-haired, slight woman who loved Denmark and had a special admiration for Anderson. As we drove through the countryside she pointed out the sights, the history, then shyly produced a book of his fairy tales and asked if she might read one to us. There were several children on board, but the adults settled down as curiously as the children to hear the story as she told it in her charmingly accented English. It was a story I had never heard before, and it entranced all of us, from the three year old to two seventyish sisters traveling together.

Here, in the world of little white houses with storks nesting on the chimney tops, thatched roof farms and wooden shoes, moated castles and mermaids, you are carried back almost 1000 years in history. A fun stop is the big ferry that holds hundred of cars and buses where you disembark to eat lunch in the restaurant as the ferry crosses the Great Belt on the journey to Nyborg, where a visit is made to Nyborg Castle, the oldest in all Scandinavia, built in 1170. There are many sights along the way, but one of the most impressive is Eageskov, one of Denmark's most beautiful manor houses, built in 1550 on oak piles rammed into a lake bed. The red walls and towers are mirrored in the water surrounding them, and if you listen carefully you might hear the moans of the daughter walled up in the castle by her stern father. The landscaped grounds are magnificent, and a well-worth stop.

Our first overnight stop was Odense, where Hans Christian Anderson was born, and where there is a remarkable museum containing his personal belongings including his top hat, umbrella, his famous rope, manuscripts and murals depicting his life. We stayed at the Grand

Hotel, comfortable, even luxurious for such a small town. On the second day we crossed the Little Belt Bridge spanning the strait between Funen and the Jutland peninsula. Lunch time found us in Ribe, Denmark's oldest town, founded in 948, where we saw many storks nesting on the roofs of the beautiful old houses. That night we stayed at a very modern hotel in Vejle, the Hotel Australia, given its name by a man who spent some time in Australia and returned to his native town to establish this tall, beautifully serviced hotel.

The tour ended on the third day at Aarhus, Denmark's second largest city, a seaport and industrial center that combines the medieval with the 20th century. Aarhus is famed for its open-air museum in the "Old Town" section, picturesque with its narrow cobblestone streets. Here are approximately fifty buildings representing Danish life from the 16th century, assembled from all parts of Denmark in their natural setting. Our hotel was the Royal, my room was enormous and well furnished, my bathroom larger than most people enjoy.

For those of us taking the three day tour, this was the end of the fairy tale trip, and we flew back to Copenhagen the next day. Others taking the four day tour continued on to Aalborg where passengers could transfer to Gothenburg, Sweden, or Oslo, Norway. However, there are direct overnight connections by boat, train and plane to Copenhagen. The three day tour from Copenhagen, including all sightseeing, hotels, meals and bus, is $77 per person, based on two sharing a room. The four day tour is $81. Children adore the trip, adults are charmed and togetherness is more than just a word as the wonderful country of Hans Christian Anderson comes alive.

The Sun Hunters Club

SOME PEOPLE HUNT GAME, others like to stalk polar bears. Me, I joined the Sun Hunters Club and found myself hunting the sun, the midnight sun, north of the Arctic Circle. Imagine a full blazing red ball of a sun at midnight, in this land of no-night, where it is daylight at one o'clock in the morning. Imagine the unbelievable specter of a sun that never sets, growing red and redder as it approaches the horizon, then lingers for a moment and now reborn is ready to start the day again.

We were on an excursion flight, one I never thought existed anywhere anymore. Usually a plane ride is taken to eliminate distance and get you where you are going as quickly as possible. But this time we deliberately took our time on this flight out of Oslo, Norway, across rich and fertile farmland. If there was something of interest down below we would circle around it. Time was unimportant. We were out to see everything worth seeing. Below us were snow-glittering mountains on our left and complete desolation. On our right, we could see green plains and signs of habitation.

As I Was Saying

Here, too, were the giants of Jotunheimen, the home of the Norwegian trolls, those enormous giants who live in the mountains and forests. Trolls, they say, are so big that you can see their heads above the tallest treetops when they walk in the woods. They have huge heads with enormous noses and long untidy hair. Sometimes they have two or even three heads, with only one eye, which they can take out to polish and shine so they can see better. Occasionally trolls have to share one eye between them, and then each troll has a hole in his forehead in which he puts the eye, sharing it one at a time. The troll with the eye walks in front and the others follow him. They look very rugged for they carry sticks, which are trees turned upside down so that the roots act as a handle. So it is easy to mistake a troll for a mountain.

The Norwegians believe in trolls, and when things go wrong it is believed that the troll has done it. Trolls are very powerful and full of magic, and everything that is good does them harm. You have to be very careful not to offend a troll, and we were careful on that flight, for looking down it was possible to see a troll or two, or think you did, anyway. But the trolls stayed away from us on this flight and when we passed the Arctic Circle we knew we were safe from them, even though we flew low over the Svartisen glacier, the largest in Norway, cold and forbidding.

Even here, where most people would not choose to live, we spotted isolated cottages where people live the hard way, farming a bit in the summer, fishing in the winter, so far removed from civilization as we know it, as possible. Our pilot knows we want to see everything, and he says, "You people sitting on the left side of the plane, look down to see the glacier. You people on the right side, don't worry, we'll turn the plane around and fly over it again, so you can see it." And he does. Time and time again he points out sights, for the left side, for the right side, taking his time so we can see everything. And we do, everything there is to see.

We play a game aboard our small plane, which seats no more than 35 people. Our steward has a sense of humor, and he wants us to guess at what time we will first see the midnight sun. We think, but how can we tell? Our steward urges us to think. Think he says, and then there it is and one of our group has guessed accurately and wins the prize. It is a tea towel, with a map of the area imprinted on its surface. He is elated. We have spotted the sun, and we are now approaching Bodo, the important communication center in Northern Norway. It is one o'clock in the morning, but it is daylight, and while some people sleep others are walking about, some tending their gardens, some just sitting around as though it was in the middle of the afternoon.

As I Was Saying

We are whisked by car to an observation chalet at Ronvikljellet for a reindeer steak dinner. But first we stand on the shore of the lake to watch the midnight sun dip down beyond the horizon, then quickly rise again. It is a magical sight. The sun was there, then gone, then here again. We are invited into the chalet where we are served our promised reindeer steak dinner. We eat while watching the full disc of the glowing midnight sun. On the horizon to the north, we see the impressive cliffs of the Lofoten Islands, and it seems natural to drink champagne and eat our reindeer steak while the midnight sun tends to its business of lighting up the earth. Here grow the lundenberries, which have been whipped into a dessert. While we eat, it seems perfectly natural to be entertained by folk dancers doing steps native to Laplanders. Everything unreal to our real world is accepted here as natural, and even the trolls are believable in this fantasy world of nature.

We have come in June, toward the last of the month. In another week the whole disc of the midnight sun will no longer be visible in its entirety. Our timing is perfect, and our memories will retain forever this scenic wonder of the world. Now it is time to return to Oslo. We are taken back to our plane, which has patiently been waiting for us. We had left Oslo at seven o'clock the night before. It is now after five a.m. the next day. Our thoughtful steward understands. He tells us stories, then says we are to nap. He knows we are tired. He will sing to us, he says, and he does. He croons to us, a Norwegian lullaby. Most of us nod off, and then he wakes us up, for we are back in Oslo. It is now 7 a.m. We have been away twelve hours on a journey to another world. We return to our hotel to sleep, perhaps to dream about the trolls.

Film Magic

IT WAS A PALACE! It was a fairy tale castle. It was a marvel of architecture and interior design. It was the movie house of my youth, the place people went to for personal pleasures and to escape the drudgery of their everyday lives. Growing up in New York City, I can remember when Radio City Music Hall was built. It was a miracle, we thought. People came by the thousands, lining up to buy tickets, and sometimes the lines extended for blocks. They came to see the films, of course, but it didn't really matter what the movie was. The Rockettes were there, with every show, sometimes appearing five times a day. There was usually a theme for the stage show and the Rockettes closed the show with their precise dancing, kicking their legs high, even higher, the shorter girls at the end, the taller ones in the middle. Always in step, beautifully costumed, accompanied by an orchestra that rose out of the depth of the theatre. Then there was the massive lobby. Even the ladies' room had to be viewed. New York had never seen anything like that.

Even neighborhood cinema houses had interesting interiors. My neighborhood movie house had star-strewn skies, painted domes, walls festooned with gold lighting fixtures that faded to a dim glow as the curtains parted and the screen came into view. Movie night was a big night out, a night we looked forward to all week long, not just for the film alone, but because it was an occasion. There was usually a double feature, plus a short animated film. There was the news of the week, and sometimes a travelogue where we sailed away with the setting sun. There was never any commercial advertising, though, but we did see coming attractions. A night out was a night out, and a movie night out lasted for hours.

Some theatres had vaudeville. How I loved it, what fun it was. I would pay my fifty cents and find a seat as close to the stage as I could. There were usually five acts, and the headliner would come on next to the last act. He might be a comedian, or there might be a song and dance act. I remember the Ritz Brothers, seemingly having as much fun doing their act as the audience had watching it. The chorus girls might have runs in their hose, or their make-up might be garish, but this was their world and they were letting us have a peek in. They let the audience into their magic world. Some of the better entertainers started their careers in vaudeville and graduated to television. Some of them went on to appear in films, but most ended up on the Ed Sullivan show, and when he died so did vaudeville.

As I Was Saying

Some of the films we saw have become classics. Who can ever forget "Gone With The Wind" or "An American in Paris"? Who can ever forget Fred Astaire and his fabulous dancing? Who could forget Gene Kelly or Clark Gable. The so called stars today twinkle for a moment, but Bob Hope, Bing Crosby live on long after their great moments on screen. The Marx Brothers, Laurel and Hardy are still remembered. We need more Lucille Balls, more Carol Burnetts, not angry comedians who try to shock with four letter words. When have you come out of a theatre lately humming some of the melodies you heard in a film? Remember "The Sound of Music"? We're still singing those tunes. "My Fair Lady", still watchable, still hummable. Has there been anything like that lately? Hollywood majors in film-violence, tries to make a star overnight, then he/she is dropped for the next one. A little more glamour, a little more of the old time movies would be more than welcome now.

Today there's not much glamour in going to the movies. When we go we sit in a small room, a room that feels like a box. Are we in box #1, 2, 3 or 4? The larger theatres have been closed down. There is no longer that feeling of magic. We select a film that still seems to have retained a bit of magic for film buffs. The stars are no longer in the skies of my local cinema. They are live, once a year, on the red carpet in Hollywood.

Nuka Hiva
French Polynesia

THE BRIDE AND GROOM drove off in their jeep, their crowns of flowers still on their heads. The jeep had a "just married" sign tacked on the back. A string of tin cans tied on to the rear of the car jangled noisily as they drove along the dusty road.

The maid of honor followed on her motor scooter, and some of the other members of the wedding party followed on their cycles. We were on the island of Nuka Hiva, in the French Marquesa Islands. Nestled in a cove of the Pacific Ocean, Nuka Hiva abounds in scenic beauty and little else.

The busiest place on the island was the post office, where a line of people from the cruise ship had formed to buy stamps and mail their cards and letters back home. Native children gathered flowers and handed them out to passing tourists. Unlike most islands I have visited, these children did not ask for or seem to expect anything in return. Not many cruise ships visit Nuka Hiva, and we seemed to be curiosities to the natives. I was given several blossoms and asked what they

As I Was Saying

were. "Eebees cus," said the little dark haired beauty. Then I recognized that of course these were hibiscus. I had no money with me, certainly no French Polynesian coins. The youngster shrugged. It really didn't matter.

There are no planned tours on Nuka Hiva, not even by the cruise ships who usually have tours in almost every port. But here there is not much to see, except for the beauty of the land and the sea. Walk down the dirt road, and where it forms a fork you turn to the right. There is the church, a focal point of the island and a building of rare beauty. There are carved figures both inside and outside the church, sculptor unknown but highly talented. Inside the church a native woman kneels praying, in an atmosphere of serenity. We tip-toe away so as not to disturb her. Nearby a choir is rehearsing, their voices wafted away in the gentle breeze.

We return from the church to the main road and reach the fork, then turn to the left. Here is a bit of park land containing many "tikis", or carved figures. Are they men? Are they women? We do not know, and no one we ask seems to know what these figures represent. Furthermore, few on the island care. It is hot, it is peaceful. No one is in a hurry. All is quiet in this little French Polynesian town where no one runs, for there is no place one has to hurry to. There is always tomorrow. There is plenty of time to do nothing.

Moorea, French Polynesia

THERE IT WAS. BALI H'ai! The slim peak with its nose turned skyward. I almost expected Bloody Mary to appear singing her song. Here was a marvel of scenery with lush tropical growth, a true Eden on earth. And yet it is so very hot. Hot and humid. But we are on holiday and can take it easy.

We had landed on the shores of Moorea, truly one of the most beautiful islands in the world. Is there a beauty contest for islands? Will Bora Bora win? Would you vote for Bali? No, Moorea it is, all 35 miles of it. Drive around the island, as we did, in a mini bus, along dirt roads which threatened to break every spring in our bus. Look at Bali H'ai, surrounded by ever present clouds. Who can forget South Pacific? Although the film was actually made in Hawaii the sequences of Bali H'ai were shot here in Moorea.

Listen to our driver, Edna. Edna is a husky Polynesian, but none of us can figure out if Edna is a man or a woman. We try to guess. We are not sure. Edna, of course, is a girl's name, but this Edna has a strong almost masculine face, and a sturdy body with legs like tree trunks. One of our passengers is bold. He says to Edna, "We think you are a very pretty girl." Edna blushes and thanks us. The puzzle is solved.

There are some 5,000 people living on Moorea today, and the pace is sleepy to slow. In the past there were many more, but diseases brought in by the white man killed off many thousands. Tourism is a mainstay of the island and although some cruise ships do put in at Moorea, they only average perhaps three or four a month. However, a number of tourists do come over from Tahiti, just fifteen miles away from Papeete. They usually spend a few hours here, then return to Tahiti the same day. There is a shuttle boat which sails several times a day and charges $7 one way, or one can fly over for $50 return fare from Papeete to Moorea in just a few minutes.

Sloping down the mountainside next to Bali H'ai, you can see pineapple seedlings that have been planted down the hillside. Edna points out the various leaves and trees, the mangos, papaya, the exotic flowers growing wild. One, a type of hibiscus, is unusual. It never opens its flowers and is seemingly asleep, but is quite alive. Edna knows this. She knows them all. We are taken to a place where sacrifices of humans were made many years ago. Heads were chopped off then. But not any more, Edna tells us. We are relieved.

There is no industry on Moorea, outside of tourism. There are a few places that sell the famous Black South Sea Pearl, a glorious costly gem. We meet Stephane LaBaysse, who tells us he is a Baron. Stephane sometimes dives for the pearls, but mostly he designs and creates magnificent jewelry to match the beauty of the pearls. Although he has a small studio in Moorea he finds it easier to sell his jewelry in Tahiti, for too few people come to Moorea to provide an income for him.

Apart from a few hotels on the island, there is a Club Mediteranee where you can live in luxury huts. There are no towns as such, only settlements. It is truly fitting that the Black South Sea Pearl is found here, for Moorea is a pearl in the heart of French Polynesia, in a setting magnificent to behold.

The Fabulous Rhine

A TRIP DOWN THE fabulous Rhine River is a must for all travelers to Germany. The famous castles appear like a scene out of Disneyland come alive, and cameras click like mad trying to capture the beauty of the scenery. When the Lorelei comes into view, the old German song is played over the loud speaker, and everyone on board finds himself singing the words, in German if he is a linguist, or just humming the enchanting tune.

Remembering the Rhine conjures up quite another vision for me. The day I took the trip was bright and sunny, and the boat was filled with only a few tourists, but mostly with Germans looking forward to a day's outing. Wandering through the boat I first heard, and then made my way toward a huge table crowded with women singing German songs with more enthusiasm than talent. They beckoned and I stopped beside them, delighted with their enthusiasm and envying their fun. Suddenly they stood up, and arms encircled about each other's waists, drew me into their circle. I was one with them. It mattered not that I didn't know the words or even the melodies of most of their songs. They sensed that the spirit was willing!

We swayed to and fro, singing with gay abandon, sisters under the skin.

A little later I had reason to pass their table again. They had risen and were forming a line, hands on the shoulders of the person ahead. I was literally pulled into the group, silly sun hat perched atop my head. The leader took it from me, put it on and urged me to the head of the line. We snake-danced around the boat, German-conga style, until most of the passengers had joined us. A trio of musicians followed, hastening our pace. Sheer, delightful madness, down the Rhine! And I never did get my sun hat back.

Cairo

HODA IS A CULTURED modern Egyptian woman, sophisticated and modern as tomorrow. She hates Cairo, where she was brought up, and now lives by choice in Alexandria. But she is a guide and given the task of taking us to Cairo when our cruise ship docked in Alexandria. As we drove through the Delta and passed villages where poverty was only too evident she explained that the poor, in Egypt, would always continue to have many children, for this was the only way they could earn money, by renting the children out to landowners to help with the crops. The money the children earned helped to sustain the family.

As we approached Cairo, we were warned not to take any pictures. Soldiers guarded the bridges in the center of the city, sandbags piled high at each end. The city of eight million people was a bustling metropolis, streets filled with pedestrians, traffic at a crawl, drivers leaning on their horns, a nightmare of confusion.

The highlights of this day were to be the museum, the Pyramids and the Sphinx, and dinner at the Nile Hilton complete with floor show featuring, naturally, a belly dancer. It was over 90 in the shade when we pulled up at the museum, which contains a remarkable assemblage of Egyptian antiquities, including ancient tombs, priceless jewels and King Tut's possessions. But the museum was crowded with tourists and after several hours we left to visit the famous pyramid of Kheops and the Sphinx.

Hoda has warned us that the Pyramids were very close to the center of Cairo. In fact, she said, in a short while the Pyramids would actually be in the center of Cairo, for the city was spreading out. New buildings were being constructed and would soon outdistance the Pyramids. But for all that warning, it seemed incredible that we had driven less than ten minutes and there they were, the three Pyramids known to most people around the world. Nearby was a hotel, with yet another soon to be built. As we left our bus, the magic of the Pyramids vanished. Here were the Arab peddlars selling their wares.

"Lady, buy this bracelet, I make you good price. Good luck to you," said the first. The bracelet was ugly and brassy looking. I didn't want it, nor had I come to buy anything. I had travelled thousands of miles to see the Pyramids and the sight of these hustling salesmen in front of one of the wonders of the world disenchanted me.

"Lady," said another, "take a camel ride. Only $1 for you. For $2 I take your picture with your camera."

I said I would think about it and turned my attention to the Pyramids. Of the three, the largest, built for Kheops, is possible to enter. Hoda advised us not to try. One must crawl on hands and knees up a long narrow corridor only to at last come into an empty chamber. People who did this later said they had sore legs for days after. A new discovery near the pyramids has revealed a ship, supposedly built to help Kheops get about in the next world. The ship is being restored and, at this writing, is not open to the public, but is housed in a shed.

The Sphinx was a distance away, so I turned to the camel vendor. Yes, I would ride his camel. The beast was uninterested and rudely continued chewing as I climbed up on the saddle. Suddenly the earth swayed as the camel started to rise. Backward I went, then forward as he stood up tall. And I mean tall. I felt higher above the earth than I do in a plane at 35,000 feet. The camel started to move, taking me with him. I thought I could indeed grow accustomed to this. Then he started down a hill and forward and down I went with him. No worse than a roller coaster, really. When the ride was over I gave the owner his money. It had been fun. But he wanted double the going price. I explained that our guide has said to pay no more.

He argued, I smiled back and said no, sweetly but firmly, I thought. He scowled, muttered something, then said in English "You are stupid."

Stupid I may have been, but not enough to buy the souvenirs, postcard, show horns and whips being hawked on the sight of this majestic reminder of a world long gone. On we went to the Sphinx and now the entire picture was perfect.

After dinner, we returned to our ship by the desert road, past huge sand dunes, mile after mile of loneliness. It was a moonlit night and we drove without headlights. Occasionally in the desert one could sight a few small tents. It was cold outside, comfortable in the bus. No buildings, no people except the occasional Bedouin, no lights, just the magic of the moon. An enchanting end to an unusual day in Egypt.

Calico Ghost Town (California)

WE WERE THREE HOURS out of Los Angeles, in the foothills of the Calico Mountains, when we came upon the old ghost town of Calico. It was named for the multi-colored mountains behind the town, but some thought it was called Calico because it was "purty as a gal's calico skirt."

Back in the 1880's, Calico was in its glory with a population of 4,000 and more than 20 saloons. It had the richest strike in California history and on Saturday nights it bristled with miners, dance hall girls, shopkeepers and gun slingers. Silver was king and Calico thrived. Some mines produced 13 to 20 million dollars in high grade ore. The find at Calico was the most valuable silver ore discovery ever recorded in California history. In just over a decade, 86 million dollars in silver ore and 9 million dollars in borax had been removed from Calico.

The prosperity brought many prospectors to town, and even though it was twice partially destroyed by fire it sprang back again. Then in 1896, the price of silver fell from $1.31 to 63 cents on ounce. Most of the miners moved on. Calico became a ghost town.

In 1951, William Knott, known for his Knott's Berry Farm in Southern California, heard about Calico and decided to restore it as it had been in its heyday. The restoration was planned from photos of Calico as it had been once. And in 1963, Knott presented Calico Ghost Town to the San Bernadino County Regional Parks Department. Today you can walk through the tunnels of some of the mines, or swap tall tales with an early prospector. There are stores and restaurants. You can boo the villain at the town playhouse and even have your portrait taken. On weekends actors act out skits in the same place where Wyatt Earp once stood.

When we entered Calico, our bus was stopped by an old man holding a gun. He ordered the doors open and climbed aboard. He announced that he was "Lonesome George" and said he would not tolerate any kind of misbehavior while we were in Calico. He twirled his gun, looking at us ferociously, then said he had heard that one of the passengers on our bus was known to be a bad 'un. It was an arranged joke between our bus driver and Lonesome George. The bad 'un was brought forward and handcuffed briefly.

Wandering around Calico can be great fun. The food is good and inexpensive. Jewelry and clothing, as well as souvenirs can be purchased. There are special celebrations three times a year; the weekend before Easter when there is a wild Pitchin', Cookin' and Spittin' Hullabaloo. Then on Mother's Day weekend in May you can win an apple pie for singing, or just enjoy barbershop, bluegrass or country music. On Columbus Day weekend in October, it's Calico Days with horse parades, a burro run and National Gunfight Stunt Championships.

Calico was born in 1881 and died in 1907. But it is very much alive now.

Watch that Watch

THE WATCH WAS BEAUTIFUL, with a tiny circlet of diamonds. The gold band attached to the watch fastened with a tiny catch, topped with a single diamond. It looked expensive, and if it was real it would have been. But it was a knock-off, a perfect reproduction of a watch she had seen recently at Tiffany's. Marcia had seen the watch when she visited the flea market and had had her brilliant idea then and there. Her mother's birthday was coming up soon, and she wanted something very special for her mother for this was to be her 65th birthday, marking her entrance into the so-called "golden age".

Marcia had been worried about the proper gift. After all, her mother had always considered herself a most proper person, dressing the "proper" way, attending the "proper" concerts, joining the "proper" clubs, maintaining friendships with the "proper" people, even if she did not always enjoy these relationships.

Marcia's father had died six years ago, and even though she had tried to suggest that her mother meet, even date, other men, her mother thought this would not be proper. Often lonely, she sat at home watching TV rather than try to meet anyone outside of her small circle of friends. Marcia, looking ahead, could see her mother growing older and sadder, utterly dependant on her daughter and grandchildren. She shuddered at the prospect. A little shaking up, she thought, was what her mother needed.

"Well," she thought, "I'll start with the watch. She'll never know it isn't real diamonds and solid gold. That's what she is used to. All her jewelry is solid gold, plain and proper, absolutely proper, nothing to offend anyone. She doesn't know that we don't have much money now, since Peter is giving up his job to go into business for himself, we haven't told her that yet. She'll just assume we can afford it. In fact, we can't. So this will have to do."

Marcia took special care in wrapping the watch, using gold paper and a diamente cord she had purchased. She composed a poem, extolling her mother's virtues and values accumulated during her lifetime. At the surprise dinner party for her mother, she brought out the gold package and watched her mother open it. The delighted expression on her mother's face was enough to repay Marcia for the trouble she had taken. Her mother's "how beautiful this is" delighted Marcia and Peter.

Estelle Craig

It was barely a week later that Marcia received a phone call from her mother. "Darling, this lovely watch must be very valuable. Don't you think I should get it insured in case I lose it?" Marcia was beside herself with worry. How could she insure this inexpensive trinket, this knock-off of a really good watch? Quickly she said, "Oh, Mother, you're always so careful. I'm sure you won't lose it."

"Well, darling, I didn't want to say, but I think there is something wrong with the clasp. It doesn't fasten too well." With a sense of relief Marcia said, "I'll just take it back and have them fix it. Then we can think about the insurance." Quickly she raced over to her mother's apartment, took the watch and went to Tiffany's, where she wrote out a check for the original, expensive watch she had first seen. No matter that it almost wiped out their savings account. No matter that they would have to budget even more carefully from now on. The important thing was that her mother would have the original, the proper watch. She deserved it.

Two weeks later Marcia told her mother that the insurance on the watch had been arranged. And how was she enjoying it? "Well, to tell you the truth, I really liked the first catch on the watch, before you had it fixed. I thought it looked so much nicer."

Around the World on the Queen Mary 2

THE HILLS WERE ALIVE with the sound of people cheering as the Queen Mary 2 came into sight in the San Francisco harbor and headed for the Golden Gate bridge. Thousands of people lined both sides of the bridge, and every available standing spot was occupied by men, women and children, anxious to see this ship, the largest ocean liner in the world. I, too, stood on the banks of the river, but later that day I would be on the ship, for I was one of the passengers on this, the maiden voyage of the Queen Mary 2, on its first round-the-world voyage. The Queen Mary 2 is a huge ship, carrying over 2500 passengers. But only some 450 have signed up for the entire voyage around the world, lasting 80 days.

Most of the passengers have purchased segments, some lasting any where from a week to several weeks. I will be on board for 52 days, and will visit Hawaii, Pago Pago, New Zealand, Australia, Hong Kong, Singapore, Malaysia, India, Dubai, Rome, France and Southampton, before taking the transatlantic voyage back to Florida. There is great excitement, both on shore, and on the part of us, the new passengers boarding the ship

Estelle Craig

The grand lobby is indeed grand, encompassing two decks in the center of the ship. There are twelve decks, and each one is one-sixth of a mile long. You do a lot of walking when you are on the Queen Mary. There are twelve different restaurants on board, and although you have your assigned table, you can choose to take your meals at one of the other restaurants, if you like, although one charges $30.00 cover charge per person. There is a planetarium, with four different shows; there is a huge spa, three swimming pools, many bars and lounges, and of course a casino filled with the usual gambling tables and loads of slot machines, ranging from five cents to dollars. There is also a large theatre where shows are presented nightly. I budget myself to $10.00, for my fling at the slots, and am prepared to lose. So I was surprised to find myself on a winning streak the first time I tried a machine I thought looked friendly. I came away with $128 and couldn't believe my luck. That carried me through the other nights when I didn't win anything.

While San Francisco greeted the QM2 so warmly, when we arrived in Honolulu there was hardly a stir. The city went about its business as though this enormous ocean liner wasn't there. And the same with out next port, American Samoa. But the tables turned in Aukland. The city went wild with excitement. People lined the shores, the streets were filled with traffic, people coming down to see the ship. We only had part of a day in Aukland, then set sail for Sydney. Due to its huge size, 1132 feet long, 148 feet wide, we were unable to lay anchor near the opera house, and had to berth out of the city. It didn't matter, though, because we were able to visit a historic moment when the Queen Elizabeth 2 came sailing by that afternoon, the two Queens saluting each other. Everyone went crazy, ship's horns were blown, fireworks were displayed, and anyone with a boat, big or little took to the water and stayed with the Queen Mary until we sailed away that evening. Traffic was so heavy in Sydney, due to the interest in the two ships, that some of our passengers had great difficulty getting back to the ship in time for our sailing to the next port and we were delayed almost three hours in sailing away.

Hong Kong was our next port, and again, because of its size, the QM2 had to anchor a distance away from the usual berth. Since we were due to sail away early that evening we had to make every moment count while we were on shore. The boats, the helicopters, the people who came to see the ship, made this visit memorable, and most of us gathered on the decks to see the lights of the beautiful Hong Kong harbor as we sailed away. Then it was Singapore, where I made a beeline for the Raffles Hotel, which I had visited years ago. How things change! It is now a large, modern hotel, with many shops. When I was there last I had bought a Raffles hat. Naturally I had to buy a new one. In truth, I liked the old Raffles better. It had charm and a certain atmosphere that this new style lacks.

Then it was back to the ship for an early sail away. Malaysia was our next port, and we toured Kuala Lumpur, visited their new mall, and then back to the ship. The only port where we stayed over night was Cochin, India. No one seemed to know why this small port was chosen for our only long stay, two days and one night. But we found it delightful, mostly due to a taxi driver we found, a man named Johnson. Once we were in his cab, a doorless tiny vehicle with rusty tires, he virtually adopted us for the day. He entered shops with us, carried our packages, and when we decided to take an air conditioned car, for it was very hot, Johnson abandoned his cab and came with us. He stayed with us all day and gave us a tearful embrace when we left to board the ship.

We're now on our way to Dubai, and most of us are excited to be visiting this port. We have heard about this exotic city, built on sand, and we are anxious to see what they have done. They have done plenty. The leaders of the United Arab Emerites have made an extensive effort to attract tourists, and indeed the tourists do come. Prices charged are exorbitant; lunch at the big hotel is $295.00 and sold out. Prices are out of reach, yet the old remains in contrast to the unusual and extremely modern buildings that have been erected We visited their new, very modern mall where people were skiing on slopes made of snow. Yet the mall was built on sand. There are modern and ancient souks, and the merchandise varies from saris to pot holders. If you have more money than you know what to do with, you can buy an island for several million dollars. A special sales office has been provided for this and it is very elegant. We visited but did not buy. In Dubai we had the pleasure of the company of Adjir, who accompanied us, in his cab, and on foot when we shopped.

Our next port was Alexandria, Egypt, and most of the QM2 passengers were eager to visit there. However the waters were so rough that morning that the port was closed to all ships. No Alexandria for us. No Cairo, no pyramids. After a thoughtful few hours of waiting, the Commodore decided to move on to our next port, Rome. Bypassing Egypt gave us an extra few hours in Rome, and most of us took advantage of this, seeing the sights, shopping, etc. Then back to the ship for LeHavre where we had several options. Do we take the long ride into Paris, or do we take a tour of the countryside? We chose to visit Normandy where we wound up at a Benedictine Monastery and were given samples of their excellent liquor.

Our last port was Southampton, and while many passengers departed from the ship, many new passengers embarked for the transatlantic voyage to its starting point, Ft. Lauderdale, Florida, where the inaugural maiden voyage of the Queen Mary 2 started. This was to be its first and last round the world trip, for the new Queen Victoria will take over in 2008. The QM2 will only do transatlantic and Caribbean trips from now on.

In Southampton, we decided to visit Windsor Castle and found a friendly guide who led us around, back stairs, front stairs, and who sang me "Happy Birthday" for it really was. Then it was off to Ft. Lauderdale, and the end of our trip. We had sailed around the world in less than 80 days. But we had so little time in each port that left many of us wondering whether indeed we had seen enough of each country. At least we know now where we want to return to see more, and where we think we have seen enough so we don't have to go back.

CPSIA information can be obtained at www.ICGtesting.com
Printed in the USA
LVOW040755270312

274955LV00001B/1/P